Ali and Amina
stories
Stage 5

Name

Match the letters.

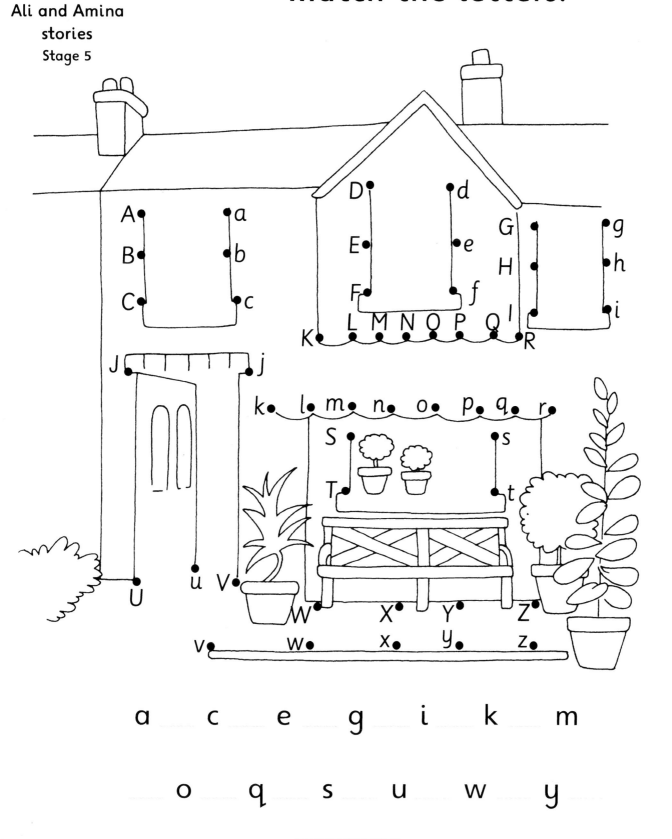

a   c   e   g   i   k   m

o   q   s   u   w   y

Heinemann

Grandma's surprise

Skill: Alphabetical knowledge – upper and lower case
Instructions: Draw a line from the capital letter to the lower case letter and complete the picture. Then fill in the missing letters in the alphabet.

Spell the word.

	his	that	come	over
Copy				
Cover the word.				
Write				
Write				
Write				
✓ or ✗				

	made	your	with	under
Copy				
Cover the word.				
Write				
Write				
Write				
✓ or ✗				

Grandma's surprise

Skill: Spelling sight words.
Instructions: Copy the first word. Cover the word with a ruler. Write the word from memory. Check the word. Repeat for the rest of the words.

Fill in the gaps.

Grandma sat in _____ garden.

She was _____ .

'I _____ we had a mango tree here,'
she said.

'I wish Grandma _____ have a mango tree,'
said Ali.

Grandpa, Ali and Amina _____ to the market.

Grandpa _____ a bag of mangoes.

Ali and Amina _____ the mangoes in the tree.

'Now I have a mango tree,' said Grandma.
She was _____ happy.

The mango tree

Skill: Reading comprehension – cloze
Instructions: Look back at the story. Then complete the sentences using the words from the mango tree.

Circle the last letter.

m r t

n s b

m g y

pot

t b f

h g n

c x h

p h c

n s x

b t d

The mango tree

Skill: Phonological awareness – final letter sounds
Instructions: Look at the object in each shopping basket. Circle the letter which makes the sound at the end of the word. Then write the whole word.

Yes or no?

yes **or** no

Was Grandpa in the garden?

Did Grandpa like the hole?

Did Ali and Amina have
a bucket?

Did Ali and Amina make
the hole?

Did Ali and Amina see a badger?

Did the badger make the hole?

Who did it?

Skill: Reading for meaning and story recall
Instructions: Read the questions then answer **yes** or **no**. Look back at the story to help you.

5

Crosswords

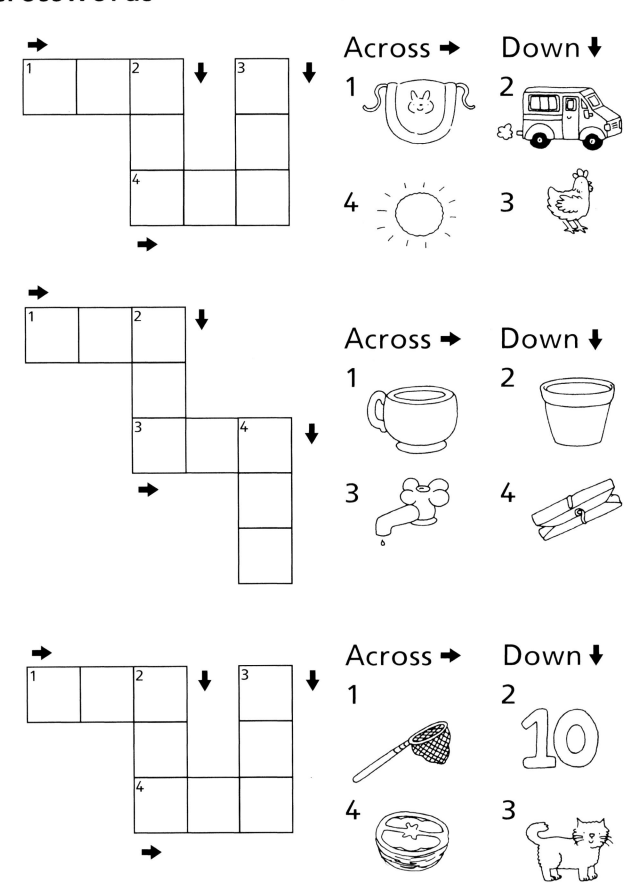

Across ➡

1   4

Down ⬇

2   3

Across ➡

1   3

Down ⬇

2   4

Across ➡

1   4

Down ⬇

2   3

Who did it?

Skill: Spelling three-letter words

Instructions: Identify the pictures and write the word in the correct place on the crossword. (Explain how the crossword clues are numbered across and down.)

Track the letters.

pa

pan top hut dot pat
bag pad pit him her
pan jet pat hen pan
did fit got pad top
man pan bad cat dog

Did you find 8?
Write 3 pa words.

pe

pen hen cat dog pet
pat peg mug hut peg
bun run hug pet fit
pan nut not pen did
vet wet peg man pet

Did you find 8?
Write 3 pe words.

pi

pin pot top got hug
pip tin men pit cup
dog pip him his pit
kit mat pin not pop
pan pit rot pip dip
bit did

Did you find 8?
Write 3 pi words.

Presents

Skill: Identifying letter patterns
Instructions: Circle all the words with the specified letter pattern. Check that you have found 8 words and then write 3 different words with the same pattern.

Fill in the speech bubbles.

ISBN 978-0-435091-53-8

1

'Uncle Sami and Raza are here,' said Grandpa.

2

'I have some presents for you,' said Raza.

3

'I have a present for Grandma,' said Raza.

4

'This is for you,' said Raza

Presents

Skill: Writing sight words

Instructions: Read the sentence under each picture and then write the speech in the speech bubble.